National Museum of the Châteaux de
Malmaison
et de Bois-Préau

art
lys

Texts by:
Amaury Lefébure,
Conservateur Général du Patrimoine,
Director of the National Museum
of the Châteaux de Malmaison et Bois-Préau.

Bernard Chevallier,
Conservateur Général Honoraire du Patrimoine and former
Director of the National Museum
of the Châteaux de Malmaison et Bois-Préau.

CONTENTS

Plans

Ground floor

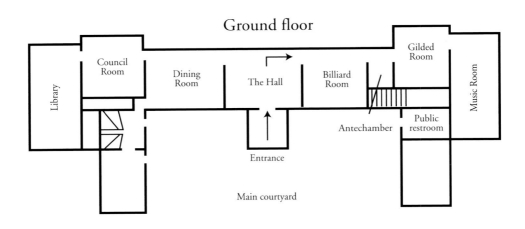

Library

Council Room

Dining Room

The Hall

Billiard Room

Gilded Room

Music Room

Antechamber

Public restroom

Entrance

Main courtyard

First floor

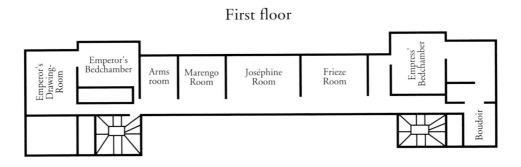

Emperor's Drawing-Room

Emperor's Bedchamber

Arms room

Marengo Room

Joséphine Room

Frieze Room

Empress' Bedchamber

Boudoir

Second floor

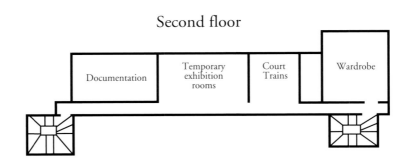

Documentation

Temporary exhibition rooms

Court Trains

Wardrobe

The library.

Introduction

Upon its acquisition by Joséphine Bonaparte in 1799, Malmaison had been a country house lying half an hour from Paris, and if it still enjoys this status today it is only thanks to its miraculous preservation made possible by the generosity of a sponsor and philanthropist, Daniel Iffla, aka "Osiris."

The origin of the name Malmaison is probably related to the Norman invasions of the 9th century when hordes of Vikings laid waste to the region during raids along the Seine from their base in Rueil. Perhaps the walls of the *mala domus* ("house of evil" in Latin) first mentioned in 1244, still echo of these turbulent times. In the early 14th century, a lord's residence is mentioned under the name "La Malmaison". It was only during the Napoleonic era, when Malmaison became the "Imperial Palace of Malmaison" that the definite article was dropped. It was purchased in 1390 by a bourgeois merchant from Paris, Guillaume Goudet, and remained in the possession of his family until 1763.

The current château was built circa 1610-1620 by Christophe Perrot (1573-1641), counsellor to the parliament of Paris who built the central structure and the pavilion of the council room. The husband of his granddaughter, Jacques-Honoré Barentin (1628-1689), himself a Parliamentarian, completed the château in 1686-1687 by building the pavilion of the Gilded Room then the two wings housing the music room and the library.

Auguste Garnerey (1785-1824), *Malmaison, seen from the gardens,* watercolour.

Pierre-Joseph Petit (working from 1795 to 1819), *Malmaison, seen from the gardens,* detail, oil on canvas, circa 1805. Right page, overall view.

As of 1737, the château was rented out to wealthy financiers before being sold in 1771 to one of the most prominent bankers in the kingdom, Jean-Jacques Le Couteulx du Molay. His wife would entertain the *crème de la crème* of the Malmaison upper society: writers, the Delille, the Baron de Grimm and Bernardin de Saint-Pierre, the Italian poet Alfieri, the famous portrait artist Mrs Vigée-Lebrun as well as modern thinkers such as the Sieyès. Around 1780, the Le Couteulx family enlarged the château by extending the courtyard façade with the addition of two short wings and then had the garden redesigned in English style.

The Revolution led them to part with Malmaison which they sold to Joséphine on April 21, 1799, in accordance with the wishes of Bonaparte (then caught up in the Egypt campaign) to acquire land near Paris. But being short on funds, she had to borrow 15,000 francs from Le Couteulx's administrator in order to put down a deposit. Upon his return from Egypt, Bonaparte finalised the purchase and became the true owner of the estate. The architects Percier and Fontaine were chosen to restore the château. In 1800, parallel to reinforcement work, they began to lay out the rooms by decorating and furnishing them in a neo-classical style of archaeological inspiration, primarily drawing on ancient Rome and Pompeii. They subsequently turned their attention to the gardens.

The First Consul and his wife were frequent visitors and would stay for several days. The château was then in its heyday. Many receptions, balls, entertainments and promenades were held here, not to mention plays performed in the small theatre in which the residents of the house would sometimes participate. Work and politics also had their place and from 1800 to 1802 Malmaison, which has a council room like the Palace of Tuileries, saw ministers frequently summoned for long meetings which would give rise to the Consulate's major

civil reforms. These repeated sejours made Malmaison the residence which Napoléon would use the most, along with the Tuileries, even though he would only occasionally visit as Emperor.

Following Bonaparte's decision to make Saint-Cloud his foremost country residence, in the autumn of 1802, Joséphine considered Malmaison as her private property and endeavoured to embellish and transform the estate which she gradually extended. She gave full rein to her passion for botany by acclimatising exotic plants for which she had built a vast greenhouse. She also introduced rare animals such as kangaroos and black swans and bred a sizeable flock of merinos in the sheepfold set up near the Saint-Cucufa pond. In 1805, she found in the architect Berthault, the man capable of producing the garden of her dreams. He created in Malmaison one of France's major landscaped garden. He also built an extensive gallery in which Josephine displayed her collection of paintings, Greek vases and sculptures.

Although she had two children from her first marriage with Viscount Alexandre de Beauharnais, Joséphine was unable to produce an heir for Napoléon who resigned himself to divorce in 1809. He left Joséphine ownership of Malmaison as well as all of its collections. Now that it was Joséphine's principal residence, she modified the apartments but piously preserved the Emperor's and particularly the library. It was in this château that she died on May 29, 1814.

Her son, prince Eugène, inherited the property but in 1828 his widow sold Malmaison to the Swedish banker Jonas Hagerman who divided up the estate. In 1842, Queen Christine of Spain, widow of the king Ferdinand VII, bought the château and stayed there during her periods of exile in France before selling it in 1861 to Napoléon III, Joséphine's grandson. Damaged by the fights during the war of 1870 then by the establishment of a barracks in the château, the estate was sold in 1877 by the governement to a merchant who gradually split up the grounds. In 1896, the financier Daniel Iffla, known as Osiris (1825-1907), purchased the château with its grounds, by then reduced to 6 hectares. He set about restoring the property before donating it to France on December 14, 1903, in order to archive the creation of a Napoleonic museum which first opened its doors to the public in 1905.

Amaury Lefébure

Façade overlooking the park;
the red marble obelisks
originated from the demolished
château of Richelieu in Poitou.

The Façade overlooking the courtyard

Instead of replacing the old residence with a neoclassical villa as they would have liked, Percier and Fontaine were forced by the First Consul to patch up the old house. The work was so great that in order to prevent the walls from giving way, they had to be supported using heavy buttresses surmounted by statues from the gardens of Marly. In 1801, the two architects added a building shaped as a tent destined to house the servants, which Bonaparte immediately described as "a booth for animals on display at the fair".

Anonymous, *View of the main courtyard*, watercolour, circa 1810.

The Façade overlooking the park

The tall slate roofs of the château reveal the influence of the architecture in the time of Louis XIII. The wall, which was originally covered with a pale yellow plaster and lime coating, was unfortunately roughcast with cement in 1937, with unsightly lines imitating geometrical cuts in the stone.

In 1807, Alexandre Lenoir, whom Joséphine appointed Curator of Objets d'Art at Malmaison, placed on the bridge above the moats two red marble obelisks which, in fact, had nothing Egyptian about them since they originated from the main door of the château of Richelieu in Poitou, commis-

Façade overlooking the park with two bronze centaurs based on the originals in the Capitole Museum in Rome.

Anonymous, *View of the château, from the park*, watercolour and gouache, circa 1802-1805.

sioned by the cardinal at the beginning of the 17th century, which had just been demolished. The décor of the façades is completed by two bronzes, a young and an old centaur, replicas of antique marbles from the Villa Adriana preserved at the Capitole Museum in Rome. The château is surrounded by moats with windows opening onto them, letting light into the basements housing the service rooms and the large kitchen built in 1687.

The Hall

The first work carried out by Percier and Fontaine was the alteration of the entrance hall. Instead of replacing the two broken upper beams, they decided to support them using four wooden posts skilfully transformed into stucco columns, thus causing the room to resemble the atrium of a Roman villa. The restoration work executed between 1991 and 1992 revealed the original delicate imitation granites, marbles and porphyry, but was unable to recreate the ingenious system of sliding mirrors placed in the central arcades, which opened the room onto the Billiard Room and the Dining-Room. The inventory drawn up in 1814, after the death of Joséphine, provided an insight into the original furniture, sold in 1829, for this particular room as well as the rest of the château. Alongside the twelve chairs by the Jacob Brothers, supplied for Murat's library at the Élysée Palace, are four busts of members of the Imperial family replacing those of Roman emperors.

Joseph Chinard (1756-1813),
carrarra marble tripod
1808 Salon, topped by an antique
marble candelabra.

The Billiard Room

Already used as such according to an inventory dating from 1703, the décor of the Billiard Room was designed in 1800 by Percier and Fontaine, and replaced in 1812 by simple moulded panels surmounted by arches designed by Louis-Martin Berthault, appointed Malmaison architect in 1805. In 1994-1995, the walls regained their green colour enhanced by fine amaranth lines contrasting with the Egyptian-earth tone of the doors and shutters. The original gaming tables were replaced by a quadrille table, a bouillotte table which once belonged to Prince Eugène, and an imposing billiard table by Mathurin-Louis Cosson from the château of Bussy-Rabutin in Burgundy. The fifteen X-shaped stools covered with red Moroccan leather, together with the two semicircular gilded wood console tables, were supplied in 1808 by Jacob-Desmalter for the château's large gallery, an extension of the Music Room, which was destroyed circa 1830.

The Antechamber

This room, its imitation marble restored in 2003, was used both as an antechamber and a place to store gaming tables currently not in use in the billiard room. Although the presence of the Louis XVI-period *tric-trac* table was mentioned in 1814, the darkened wood desk reminds that of the usher on duty which was there originally. On the wall, the six portraits of the Sheiks of the Divan of Cairo were painted for the First Consul. Described as being present in the Billiard room until 1810, they were subsequently displayed in this room.

Michele Rigo (1772-1814), *Sheik Sulayman al-Fayyûmî* or *Sheik*, oil on canvas, circa 1800-1803.

The Gilded Room

The Company Drawing-Room, now called "salon doré" ("Gilde Room"), already on this site in the late 17th century, received two different types of décor, one in 1800 and the other in 1810-1811. The only remaining original decorative elements are the two large paintings on the theme of Ossian painted by Gérard (replica painted by the artist, the original was destroyed in 1945) and Girodet (original), the six mahogany armchairs adorned with Egyptian heads attributed to the Jacob Brothers and covered with blue velvet, together with the chimney piece given to the First Consul by Pope Pius VII in 1802, but which unfortunately lost its hard stone inlays following the fightings of 1871.

Attributed to the Jacob Brothers, arm of one of the chairs belonging to the original furniture commissioned for the room, mahogany and gilded wood, circa 1800.

Attributed to the Jacob Brothers, armchair originating from Joséphine's Bonaparte Room at the Saint-Cloud Palace, gilded wood, circa 1802.

Étienne-Jean Delécluze
(1781-1863), *Three scenes
from the tale of Daphnis
and Chloë*, oils on canvas,
from the décor of the Gilded
Room executed in 1810-1811.

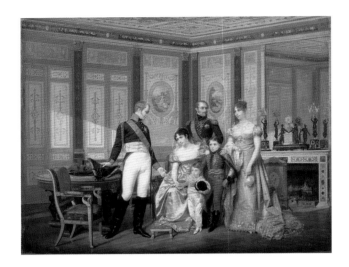

Jean-Louis-Victor Viger du Vigneau, as known as Hector Viger, (1819-1879), *Empress Joséphine entertains Emperor Alexander in Malmaison, to whom she recommends her children*, oil on canvas, 1864.

New Décor

Redecorated by Berthault during the winter of 1810-1811, while the Empress was staying at the château of Navarre near Évreux, the only remaining elements of the new décor are the ceiling, the cornice and doors together with four of the six medallions commissioned to the painter Delécluze, depicting the tale of Daphnis and Chloë. It was this décor, unfortunately extremely damaged during the war of 1870, that Viger reproduced in his painting, *Empress Joséphine entertains Emperor Alexander in Malmaison, to whom she recommends her children*. All of the chairs covered with gros de Tours originate from Joséphine's Room at the Saint-Cloud Palace.

Anne-Louis Girodet
de Roucy-Trioson (1767-1824),
*The Apotheosis of the French heroes
who died for their homeland during
the War of Freedom*; displayed
in this room from 1802 to 1810,
oil on canvas, 1800-1802.

François Gérard (1770-1837),
*Ossian conjuring up spirits with
the sound of his harp on the banks
of the Lora*; replica by the artist of
the painting displayed in this room
from 1802 to 1810, oil on canvas.

The Music Room

Like the Library, Percier and Fontaine designed this vast room over three small rooms in order to transform it into a gallery reserved for work by modern painters to whom the Empress commissioned numerous paintings. Rather than renowned artists such as David or Gros, Joséphine had a liking for the anecdotal movement, now known as troubadour painting. She was the first to start the fashion of medieval, chivalrous and sentimental subjects portrayed by painters such as Richard, Mlle Lorimier, Turpin de Crissé, Bergeret and Laurent. Her fondness for paintings of flowers should not be forgotten, the most magnificent of which are those by Van Daël. Restored in 1997-1998, the room has regained many of its "troubadour" paintings, its four armchairs and two of the four original settees, together with the splendid harp by Cousineau delivered for Empress Joséphine.

Attributed to the Jacob Brothers, one of four armchairs in the Music Room, mahogany, gilded wood, circa 1800.

Fleury Richard (1777-1852), *Charles VII writing his farewells to Agnès Sorel*, replica by the artist of the painting which used to be found in the Music Room, oil on canvas, circa 1805.

The Dining Room

A dining-room lit by four windows is mentioned on this exact site as early as 1703, which is rather unusual for the period. Percier and Fontaine would later extend it, adding the semicircular part, the floor covered with lavish black and white marble paving. They would commission a series of six Pompeiian style dancers painted on stucco to the artist Louis Lafitte, which form the main part of the décor.

Restored between 1985 and 1987, the Dining Room has rediscovered its original décor enhanced by Berthault in 1812 with wooden arches adorned with fruit on a background of grapes. The original plain mahogany furniture was sold with the rest of the furniture in 1829, and was replaced by twelve chairs and a table from the Tuileries Palace, supplemented by three console tables delivered for Fontainebleau.

Louis Lafitte (1770-1828) after Charles Percier (1764-1838), three of eight dancers painted on stucco decorating the walls of the Dining Room, 1800.

The Council Room

Bonaparte's increasing number of visits to Malmaison soon required the building of a room in order to convene the Council of Ministers. Completed over ten days in July 1800, the room was merely shaped as military tent decorated with striped twill. One hundred and sixty-nine councils were held here between 1801 and 1802. Some of the matters discussed in this room included the bill creating the Order of the Legion of Honour, the confe-

In the Council Room:
François Gérard (1777-1839),
*Letizia Bonaparte, The Emperor's
Mother*, oil on canvas, circa 1805.

François Gérard (1777-1839),
Joséphine Bonaparte, replica
of the painting executed in 1801
and preserved at the Hermitage
Museum, oil on canvas.

Jacob Brothers, from a drawing
by Charles Percier (1764-1838),
X-shaped stool from the original
furniture of the room, gilded,
patinated wood, 1800

rence on the Concordat, and the ratification of the treaty of San Ildelfonso
which returned Louisiana to France. It was also here that Bonaparte followed
the arrest and execution of the Duke of Enghien, hour by hour, in 1804.
Several gilded wood chairs covered with red cloth, some of which from the
original décor of the room, are grouped around the portraits of Joséphine and
Madame Mère.

The Library

Estabished by knocking down the partition walls of three small rooms, the Library is entirely panelled with magnificent mahogany crafted by the Jacob Brothers in 1800. The décor comprises projecting parts adorned with mirrors destined to hide the flue from the fireplace situated in the basement and a vault which, according to Bonaparte, would make the room resemble the vestry of a church! Painted the course of ten days, the ceiling displays portraits of ancient and modern authors, such as Homer and Voltaire, in medallions around figures of Apollo and Minerva. More than 500 volumes with the monogram B-P (for Bona-Parte) have regained their place on the shelves which originally held approximately 4500 volumes. The magnificent bureau, with the mechanism invented by the Jacob Brothers, was used by Napoléon in his cabinet at the Tuileries Palace throughout his reign. A hidden staircase, the entrance to which is located behind the mirrors, enabled Napoléon to make his way discreetly to his apartment on the first floor.

From to top to bottom:
Voyage de la Troade, book with the monogram of Empress Joséphine, marbled calfskin, 1799.

Attributed to Georges Jacob (1739-1814), detail of the chair said to have been used by Bonaparte at his hotel situated on rue de la Victoire, mahogany, circa 1795.

The Emperor's Drawing-Room

When they first settled at Malmaison, Napoléon and Joséphine shared a bedchamber in what is now known as the Empress' Bedchamber. However, in approximately 1803, Napoléon, who had to cross the entire château in order to reach his bedchamber from his library, decided to move his quarters to the south wing in two small rooms situated just above part of the Council Room and the Library. Now known as the Emperor's Room and Bedchamber, the two rooms were reorganised in 1969 for the bicentenary of Napoléon's birth, but without preserving the original dimensions since the rooms were then separated by partition walls and were half their current size. The room serves as a showcase for a series of paintings depicting members of the imperial family, including a portrait of Empress Joséphine by Riesener, son of Marie-Antoinette's cabinetmaker, and another of the Emperor in his coronation robes from Gérard's studio, which once belonged to Queen Hortense. The octagonal pedestal table, purchased by Napoléon III, is part of the château's original furniture.

Henri-François Riesener
(1767-1828), *Empress Joséphine*,
oil on canvas, 1806.

The Emperor's Room
after restoration, in 2013.

31

The Emperor's Bedchamber

Currently twice the size of the original bedchamber, this room was decorated in 1969 with striped white Indian silk which replaced the striped muslin described in 1814 in the inventory following the death of the Empress. While the bed by Jacob-Desmalter was delivered in 1806 for Prince Eugène's bedchamber at the Tuileries Palace, the mahogany chairs came from Saint-Cloud and were covered with yellow kerseymere cloth embroidered with black fabric motifs reproducing the original trimmings.

Louis-Albert-Ghislain Bacler d'Albe (1761-1824),
General Bonaparte, detail, oil on canvas, 1796-1797.

A bronze statue of victory, by the sculptor Chaudet, which held the statue of the Emperor at the top of the Vendôme column, stands on the circular pedestal table delivered for Murat at the Élysée Palace. The portrait of General Bonaparte, one of the oldest known, was painted by Bacler d'Albe in Milan during the first campaign in Italy at the end of 1796 or in early 1797.

The Arms Room
The Marengo Room

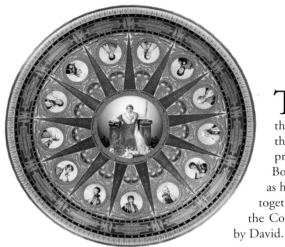

Transformed into exhibition rooms for the museum at the beginning of the 20th century, these rooms have lost their original layout. They are now used to present personal mementoes belonging to Bonaparte, General and First Consul, such as his sabres or ceremonial two-edged sword, together with distinguished works relating to the Consulate period, such as *Crossing the Alps* by David.

Details from the *Austerlitz Table* tabletop, displaying, around the figure of Napoléon, the portraits of his joint chiefs on the day of the Austerlitz battle (December 2, 1805).

Attributed to Martin-Guillaume Biennais (1764-1843): stool shaped as crossed swords (a pair), mahogany, gilt bronze, circa 1813-1814.

Manufacture de Sèvres (manufacturer), *Austerlitz Table*, designed by Charles Percier (1764-1838), portraits painted by Jean-Baptiste Isabey (1767-1855), bronze by Pierre-Philippe Thomire (1751-1843), hard-paste porcelain, 1808-1810.

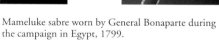

Top:
Jacques-Louis David (1748-1825),
*Napoleon Bonaparte, First Consul,
Crossing the Alps at Great-Saint-Bernard
Pass,* original commissioned
by Charles IV King of Spain,
oil on canvas, 1801.

Mameluke sabre worn by General Bonaparte during
the campaign in Egypt, 1799.

Sabre worn by General Bonaparte during the
Coup d'État on 18 Brumaire; the blade bears the
inscription "Armée d'Égypte".

Sabre worn by General Bonaparte during the first
campaign in Italy, 1796-1797.

The Joséphine Room

Built on the site of three rooms in Queen Hortense and Prince Eugène's apartment, this room displays numerous mementoes belonging to Empress Joséphine: tapestry portraits from the Gobelins Manufacture, personal objects, items of table linen, coffee and tea sets, most made of Sèvres porcelain, accompanied by a few fine examples of glassware inscribed with her monogram. The most spectacular part of the collection represents almost fifty or so pieces of two ceremonial services commissioned by the Empress and her son, Prince Eugène, to the Dihl et Guérhard porcelain factory in Paris. Taken to Munich after the collapse of the Empire, the double service was used in Saint Petersburg by the Russian descendants of the prince before being confiscated during the October Revolution. The pieces on display were sold by the Soviets between the two World Wars.

Manufacture de Dihl et Guérhard, Paris (manufacturer), top: plate belonging to a set of dessert plates commissioned by Empress Joséphine after the divorce, *View of the Church of Saint George of the Greeks in Venice,* hard-paste porcelain, 1811-1812;
Opposite: a pair of iceboxes wearing the monogram of prince Eugène, hard-paste porcelain, circa 1811-1813.

Bottom: *Manufacture de Sèvres* (manufacturer), teapot, cup and saucer from the "Cabaret égyptien" of Empress Joséphine, hard-paste porcelain, 1808.

Jean-Baptiste Regnault (1754-1829),
Queen Hortense, oil on canvas,
circa 1810.

Andrea Appiani (1754-1817),
Prince Eugène, Viceroy of Italy,
oil on canvas, 1810.

Joséphine had two children from her first marriage, at the age of sixteen, to Viscount Alexandre de Beauharnais, guillotined in 1794: Hortense Queen of Holland (she married Louis Bonaparte, brother of Napoléon), and Eugène, Viceroy of Italy, whose descendants include the present day kings of Sweden, Norway and Belgium, the queens of Denmark and Greece, the Grand Duke of Luxembourg and the Margrave of Baden.

The Frieze Room

This room occupies the bedchamber of Mlle Avrillion, the Empress' chambermaid, together with Joséphine's bathroom. The frieze with its mytho-logical subject comes from the drawing-room of the hotel purchased by Bonaparte, sat on rue de la Victoire where he lived with Joséphine until the Coup d'État in November 1799. The house was demo-lished during the Second Empire, but the frieze was removed and given to the Malmaison museum in 1961.

Anonymous, decorative frieze with a mythological subject originating from the drawing-room of the hotel situated on rue de la Victoire, oil on plaster, end of the 18th century.

Jacob Brothers, based on a design by Charles Percier (1764-1838), pedestal table from the drawing-room of the hotel situated on rue de la Victoire, mahogany, gilded bronze, circa 1796.

Attributed to Jacob Brothers, cabinet of Empress Joséphine's pageantry appartment room in the Tuileries palace, lemon-tree wood, darkened wood and ebony, circa 1798-1800.

In addition to the circular pedestal table, based on a design by Percier, and the large console table commissioned for the hotel on rue de la Victoire, this room also contains several pieces of furniture from Empress Joséphine's rooms at the Tuileries Palace, such as the yew dressing-table from her boudoir, the carpet from her bedchamber and the chest of drawers with Egyptian motifs from her private apartment.

Clock depicting Jason's conquest of the Golden Fleece, clockwork mechanism by Lesieur, gilt bronze with patina, circa 1810-1815

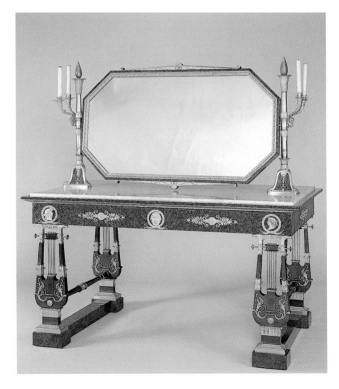

Attributed to Martin-Éloi Lignereux (1752-1809) or to Jacob Brothers, Empress Joséphine's dressing table from the Tuileries Palace, yew tree, circa 1800-1803.

Martin-Guillaume Biennais
(1764-1843), small table,
which stood on the bed,
bearing the monogram
of Joséphine Bonaparte,
with writing essentials
and toiletries, circa 1800.

The Empress' Antechamber

Fitted out in the northern part of the château in 1800, the apartment shared conventionally by the consular couple for several years became used
exclusively by Joséphine when Bonaparte decided to establish his quarters in
the south wing, just above his study and the Council Room. It access was via
this very simply furnished antechamber, which now serves to present a few
portraits of Joséphine and several objects which once belonged to her. It was in
this room, where the footmen usually stood, that the post-mortem took place
and the Empress' body was embalmed before being placed in the lead coffin.

Joséphine was a passionate col-
lector who gathered thousands
of artworks, sculptures, porce-
lains, antique or natural his-
tory items… She was helped
in this endeavour by Alexandre
Lenoir (1726-1806), a curator
from the Musée des monu-
ments français, Dominique
Vivant-Denon (1747-1825),
director of Napoléon's Louvre,
or Guillaume-Jean Constantin
(1755-1816), whom she appointed "warden of Malmaison's
paintings".

On the left:
Pierre-Paul Prud'hon (1758-1823),
Unfinished portrait of Empress Joséphine,
oil on canvas, circa 1805.

On the right:
Jean-Baptiste Vermay (1786-1833),
Mary Stuart, Queen of Scotland,
receiving the death sentence ratified
by Parliament, detail, oil on canvas,
circa 1808-1810.

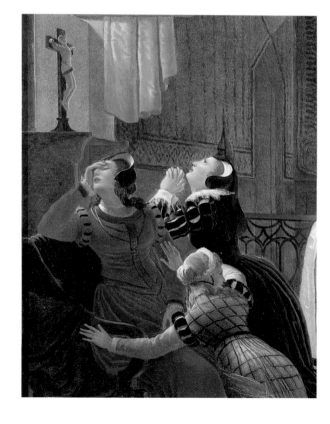

The Empress' Bedchamber

Restructured by the architect Berthault after the divorce, while the Empress travelled to Milan in the summer of 1812, this magnificent room is shaped as a tent with sixteen sides, embellished with numerous mirrors to bring in more light. The décor on the walls and the furniture, taken to Munich by Prince Eugène after the death of the Empress, were completely restored by orders of Napoléon III in 1865. Only the gilded wood bed delivered by Jacob-Desmalter in 1812 has returned to its original place. It was here that Joséphine breathed her last on May 29 1814, on the day of Pentecost, aged only fifty-one years, having succumbed to a throat infection.

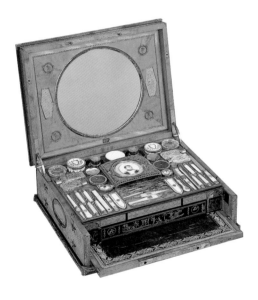

Félix Rémond, cabinetmaker (1779-circa 1860), Pierre Leplain, silversmith in 1798, Reynard Schey (1760-1816), and Vigneux, miniaturist, toiletries belonging to Empress Joséphine, 1806.

The Ordinary Bedchamber

During the Consulate when the couple shared the same bedchamber, this cabinet served as a makeshift room whenever one of them was ill. After becoming empress, Joséphine turned it into her ordinary bedchamber as opposed to her large ceremonial bedchamber, since she found this corner room better lighted and sunny. She often came here to read her botanical books or write her letters. It was in these cupboards that Joséphine kept her numerous jewels and various sets of diamonds, rubies, emeralds, opals, burnt topaz, turquoises and jets.

Martin-Guillaume Biennais (1764-1843), jewellery chest serving as a writing case, with the monogram of Joséphine Bonaparte, mahogany, steel and silver, circa 1802-1804.

The Dressing Room

Furnished with an armchair and a mahogany dressing-table with its water jug and basin made of Sèvres porcelain, the dressing room should not be confused with the dressing room: while the latter was used for washing, the dressing room was used for dressing which could be a rather time-consuming affair since Joséphine would not think twice about spending nearly three hours in here every morning.

The Boudoir

Martin-Guillaume Biennais (1764-1843), letter box with Empress Joséphine's coat of arms, mahogany, gilded bronze, circa 1804.

Always sensitive to draughts, the Empress enjoyed sitting in this octagonal room which was easy to heat due to its lowered ceiling. It could be used as a small dining-room on occasions when the Empress had only one or two guests and would sit down to eat at eleven o'clock. Half of the original chairs, the circular pedestal table on which she took her meals, together with the mahogany letter box by Biennais which was used to collect her mail, have been returned to this room decorated with muslin.

The Wardrobe

Created in 1812 following designs by Berthault, this room has retained its simple oak cupboards in which the Empress' luxurious wardrobe was kept, a few items of which still exist. Fashion was Joséphine's whole life. She created her wardrobe with the aid of her couturier Leroy, spending fantastic sums of money in the process. Exceeding even the wishes of the Emperor, who intended to develop the luxury goods trade, she had countless clothes delivered, and in just one year ordered 985 pairs of gloves, 520 pairs of shoes and 136 gowns! The Empress would visit the Wardrobe twice a year in order to inspect clothes that she wished to throw away; these were not at all worn out or torn, but generally no longer to her taste. They were then split into several groups, divided at random and shared between Madame Mère, Caroline Murat and Queen Catherine of Westphalia, together with various other chambermaids in her entourage.

Chamois leather travel blanket bearing Joséphine's monogram.

Embroidered muslin stole which once belonged to Empress Joséphine.

On the left: Lace bonnet worn by the Empress before having her hair done in the morning.

On the right: pair of fur-lined ankle boots belonging to Empress Joséphine.

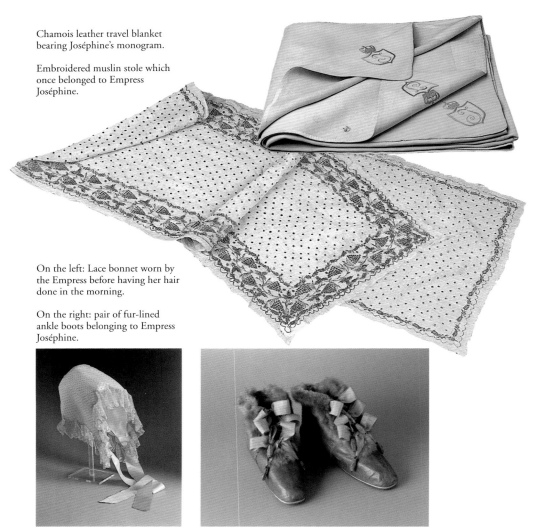

Bourrienne, Napoléon's private secretary, said of Josephine: "it was her wish to acquire and not to possess". This compulsive desire would make her very familiar with merchants who would take advantage of her absolute lack of order.

Empress Joséphine's court dress.

Court attire given to the First Consul by the city of Lyon, 1800.

Court attire belonging to François Marquis de Beauharnais (1756-1846).

Court attire worn by the senior member of the Council of State, which probably belonged to Pierre-Louis Roederer (1754-1835).

Lerebours, optician, opera glasses and case with the initial J, which once belonged to Empress Joséphine.

The Court Trains

Although the various clothes worn by Joséphine at the time of the Coronation have disappeared and are only known through the ceremonial portraits, the magnificent court robes presented here provide an insight into the lavishness of court dress. They were only worn on formal occasions and forty-nine are listed in the inventory of Joséphine's wardrobe drawn up in 1809. Generally consisting of a gown supplemented by a train, they were made from sumptuous fabrics, velvets or tulles embroidered with gold, silver or even platinum for the most exceptional trains. The Emperor would be involved in the most intricate details of Joséphine's toilet and often indicated which gowns he wished her to wear.

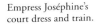

Empress Joséphine's
court dress and train.

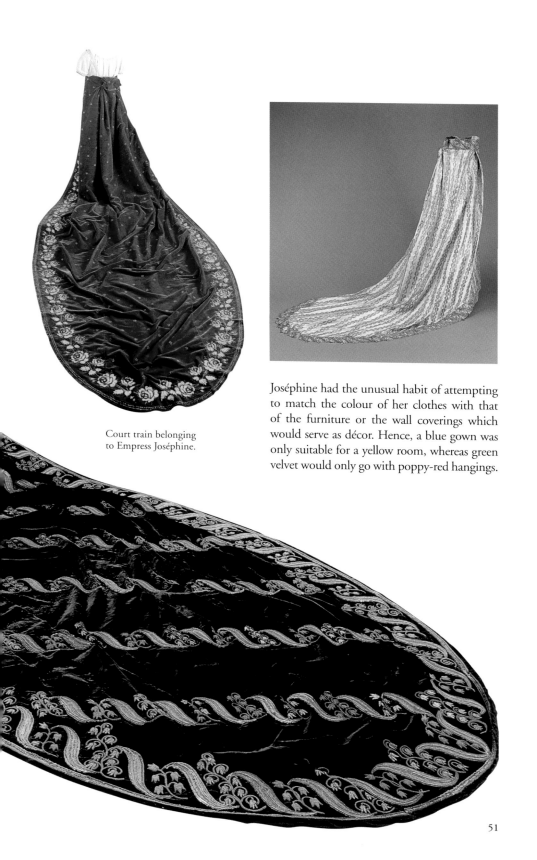

Court train belonging
to Empress Joséphine.

Joséphine had the unusual habit of attempting to match the colour of her clothes with that of the furniture or the wall coverings which would serve as décor. Hence, a blue gown was only suitable for a yellow room, whereas green velvet would only go with poppy-red hangings.

The Osiris Pavilion

Built in 1923 from the funds left to that effect by Daniel Iffla, known as Osiris (1825-1907), this pavilion also houses part of his collection of masterpieces bequeathed to France following his donation of the Malmaison domain in 1903. In addition to a beautiful series of drawings, paintings and sculptures, it also consists of Greek vases, Egyptian statuettes and several Far-Eastern items.

Albert-Ernest Carrier-Belleuse (1825-1887), bust of Michel-Ange, terracota.

Anonymous, attributed to Louis-Jean-François Lagrenée (1724-1805), *Joseph and Potiphar's wife*.

Nikosthenes, potter working in Athens, amphora with black figures, late 6th century B.C.

On the left: Édouard Bisson
(1856-1945), *Portrait of Daniel
Iffla, known as Osiris,*
oil on canvas, 1897.

On the right: Egyptian statuettes,
most of which represent the
god Osiris, 1st millennium B.C.

Alexandre Bida (1813-1895), *Salomon's wall,*
wash drawing, pencil and ink, 1857 Salon.

The Carriage Pavilion

Built circa 1830 for the owner of the time, Jonas Hagerman, these stables still retain some of the stalls and mangers. The Empress' stables, much larger, were situated outside the current domain. In addition to a number of sculptures stored for preservation purposes, the pavilion also houses three horse-drawn carriages: a *fourgon-dormeuse* (a type of carriage in which one could sleep), of no particular historical origin, by coachbuilder Devaux, the hearse used in Saint Helena for the Emperor's funeral, and, above all, the berlin landau crafted for Napoléon by coachbuilder Getting in 1812 for the French invasion of Russia. This carriage rode all the way to Moscow, and then returned to serve the Emperor until the Battle of Waterloo. It was seized by Prussian troops on June 18, 1815, stripped of its contents and awarded to Field Marshall Blücher. His descendants donated it to Malmaison in 1975.

Getting, the Emperor's field landau delivered in 1812,
used during the campaign in Russia and seized
by the Prussians at the Battle of Waterloo in 1815.

This statue adorned the temple of love raised in 1807 by the architect Berthault in the park of Malmaison. It was originally commissioned for Ms Clairon, a famous *Théatre-Français* actress, which had these two verses by Voltaire engraved on its base: "Qui que tu sois, voici ton maître: il l'est, le fut, ou le doit être !" ("Whoever you are this is your master: Past, present or future.") When the Malmaison estate was sold in 1877, the sculpture entered to the Louvre collections; it was returned to the château in 1970.

Jean-Pierre-Antoine Tassaert (1727-1788), *Cupid bending his bow*, marble, circa 1780

The park

Tirelessly extended by Joséphine, at the time of her death, the Malmaison domain reached a surface area of 726 ha and included three castlex: Malmaison, Bois-Préau and Buzenval. Completely re-landscaped by Berthault in 1805, the enclosed 70-ha park was interspersed with constructions and planted with numerous exotic shrubs. He also skilfully opened up the view of the Marly aqueduct, Saint-Germain château and the steeple of the Croissy church visible from the château. Divided up after the death of Prince Eugène in 1824, the domain only comprised 50 ha of enclosed park when it was sold by the French Governement in 1877. Gradually divided into plots, it had been reduced to 6 ha when purchased by Daniel Osiris in 1896. A majestic cedar, planted in 1800 to celebrate the Marengo victory, still stands close to the château.

Auguste Garnerey (1785-1824), *View of the wooden bridge over the river to the left of the château,* and *View of the park from the château,* watercolors.

The Gardens

Among the rare constructions still standing on the six ha of the current park is a small octagonal pavilion built in approximately 1790, which Napoléon converted into a sort of summer cabinet where he liked to work. The Temple of Love and the large greenhouse now belong to private properties. A nearby rose-garden boasts more than one hundred and ten types of ancient roses.

Antoine-Ignace Melling (1763-1831),
Malmaison park, watercolour, circa 1810.

Redouté, Joséphine and the Roses

T he name Joséphine has often been associated with roses. This reputa-
tion originates from a magnificent publication which appeared after her
death, based on drawings by her flower painter, Pierre-Joseph Redouté. Since
the old rosebushes only flowered one month in the year, they were placed in
pots and only brought out during the flowering period. Rose-gardens planted
in open ground only appeared right at the end of the 19th century.

Jean-Louis-Victor Viger du Vigneau,
known as Hector Viger
(1819-1879), *Memory of
Malmaison*, known as *The Rose
of Malmaison*, oil on panel,
1866 Salon.

Pierre-Joseph Redouté
(1759-1840), engravings taken
from *The Roses*, work published
between 1817 and 1824.

ROSA Damascena.

ROSIER de Cels

P. J. R.

ROSA Rechinata flore sub multiplice. ROSIER à boutons penches, aux à fleurs sous dou.

ROSA Damascena. subalb. ROSIER de Damas à Pétale teinté de rose.

ROSA Gallica officinalis. ROSIER de Provins ordinaire.

61

The Château de Bois-Préau

Purchased with its 17 ha park by Joséphine in 1810 in order to extend the Malmaison domain towards the town of Rueil, the château was rebuilt in 1854 for Abraham-Édouard Rodriguès-Henriquès. Donated to the National Museums by Edward Tuck in 1926, it henceforth housed an annex of the Malmaison museum dedicated to the Napoleonic legend and propaganda, together with mementoes belonging to the Emperor in Saint Helena.

Vital-Gabriel Dubray, known
as Vital-Dubray (1813-1892),
Empress Joséphine, marble, 1865.

Cover: Empress Joséphine's bedchamber.
Back cover: François Gérard (1770-1837), *Empress Josephine in Imperial costume*, oil on canvas, 1808.

Photographics credits:
National museum of the château de Malmaison and Bois-Préau: p. 59t left, 59c right; RMN-GP : p. 11, 24-25, 32-33, 51l, 51r; RMN-GP/Arnaudet Daniel : p. 6b, 7, 9, 12, 13t, 14, 15, 16, 17t, 18t, 18b, 20t, 21b, 22t, 23, 26, 27, 28b, 30, 35b (les 3), 36t, 39b, 44b, 48c, 55, 62, 63, 60t, 60b left, 60b right, 61t, 61b left, 61b centre, 61b centre; RMN-GP/Arnaudet Daniel/Schormans Jean : p. 6t, 36c, 37b, 42, 53t right, 56t, 56b; RMN-GP/Bellot Michelle : p. 13b; RMN-GP/Blot Gérard : cover, 10, 10-11, 18t (all 3), 19t (all 3), 19b, 20b, 22b, 35t, 38t, 38c, 39t, 39, 41t, 41b, 43, 46, 48 (the 2 at the top), 52t, 52b left, 52b right, 53t left, 54, 58t, 59t right, 59b, back cover; RMN-GP/Doury François : p. 4, 29, 44t, 45, 47b; RMN-GP/DR : 34t, 34b, 36b, 50l, 48t left, 58b; RMN-GP/Lewandowski Hervé : p. 53b; RMN-GP/Mathéus : p. 47t, 49t; RMN-GP/Martin André : p. 28t, 33t, 37t, 48b, 49l; RMN-GP/Martin Yann : p. 34c, 49r; RMN-GP/Raux Franck : p. 21t, 31; RMN-GP/Walter Marc : p. 38b.

Editions Artlys
Director: Séverine Cuzin-Schulte
Editor: Karine Barou
Graphic design and layout: Martine Mène and Hervé Delemotte
Production: Pierre Kegels

© Artlys, 2001
ISBN: 978-2-85495-168-4

Printed at Cesson-Sévigné (France), on October 30 th, 2013
by Edicolor Print
Legal Deposit: November 2013